The Baker

by Adri Gabriel
illustrated by Bernard Adnet

 HOUGHTON MIFFLIN   BOSTON

Printed in China

ISBN-13: 978-0-547-02018-1
ISBN-10: 0-547-02018-X

5 6 7 8 9 0940 15 14 13 12 11 10

baker

I **make** apple pies.

cherry

I make cherry pies.

peach

I make peach pies.

pumpkin

I make pumpkin pies.

I make all the pies!

Responding

TARGET SKILL **Text and Graphic Features** Pick two pictures. Tell how the words go with the pictures. Make a chart.

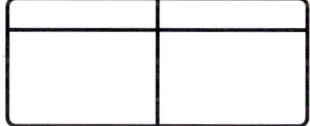

🖊 **Write About It**

Text to Self Draw a picture about something you have baked or cooked. Label your picture.

7

TARGET SKILL **Text and Graphic Features** Tell how words work with art.

TARGET STRATEGY **Summarize** Stop to tell important events as you read.

GENRE **Realistic fiction** is a story that could happen in real life.